AF480361

Dedication

*To the ones crying behind closed doors, smiling
through pain, and healing in silence—
This book is for you.
You're stronger than you know.*

A Note to the Reader

Hey,
I don't know what you're going through. I don't
know the weight you carry on your shoulders. But I
do know one thing—you're not alone. These pages
are for every broken piece, every quiet tear, every
moment you thought you couldn't keep going.
You're here. And that means you're already stronger
than yesterday. So take your time. Breathe. Feel
every word.

Healing starts here.

*Love,
Smina*

CONTENTS

"It's Okay to Not Be Okay"

Have you ever had a hundred thoughts screaming in your mind, each one different, each one louder than the last, until nothing made sense? You overthink every word, every action, and in the process, you end up doubting yourself more than you ever should. It's a feeling that can creep up on you, sometimes over something small. It could be just one fight, one disagreement, or a moment of silence that wasn't meant to be so loud. But in that moment, you realize—words hurt the most. Not because of their meaning, but because of the weight they carry when they're spoken carelessly or without thought from someone close to your heart.

Then, you start losing yourself. You begin thinking about it when you sit, when you play, when you do anything—and suddenly, you're crying. The tears fall without warning, and you don't even know why it's hurting so much. It's just there, like a lump in your chest that never really leaves. And that's okay. It really is. It's okay to not be okay. Sometimes the strongest thing you can do is let yourself feel. Cry it all out. Break down. Be real. Millions of people are silently battling their own storms, just like you. You're not weak for feeling. You're human.

I know you can't always go and tell someone everything that's tearing you apart inside. Maybe they won't understand. Maybe they'll judge. Maybe… you don't even have the words. And that's okay too. But don't bottle it all up and walk around pretending to be happy. You owe yourself more than that. You owe yourself truth. You owe yourself healing.

And you know what? At the end of the day, when the world quiets down and it's just you and your thoughts, you might feel alone. Really, truly alone. Like no one gets it. Like no one's really there. Just you, lying on a cozy bed, overthinking, remembering, breaking a little more with each thought.

But here's something real: people come into your life when you least expect them and sometimes leave when you need them the most. That's not your fault. That's life. Don't hold on to people who treat your heart like it's replaceable. Learn to let go of the ones who don't value you. Set your peace above their presence.

Because the right people—the ones who truly care—will stay. Even when you're at your lowest. Even when you're quiet, distant, or not yourself. They'll see through the silence. They'll stay for the storms, not just the sunshine.

It's not just you. I promise.

 You will feel left out. Not once, not twice—but many times. You'll sit in a group and still feel invisible. You'll watch people laugh around you, and wonder why your smile feels so forced. You'll see others form bonds, hold hands, share secrets—and you'll question why yours feel distant. It stings, doesn't it? To feel like a guest in someone else's world while you're just trying to find your place. But hear this: it doesn't mean you're not enough. It doesn't mean you're unlovable. Sometimes people are caught in their own stories and forget to notice the ones quietly writing their own. That doesn't make your story any less worthy.

You don't have to change who you are to be seen. You don't have to dim your light just to fit in. The right people will notice your silence, not just your laughter. They'll sit beside you when you feel left out, without needing to be asked. You deserve the kind of people who make you feel included just by being near them. So if you're feeling left out today, just know this—it won't always be like this. One day, you'll look around and see people who see *you*, truly and entirely. Until then, hold on. You're not alone in this feeling, and you're not forgotten.

And until they come—or if they already have—remember this: you are enough, even when you feel like a mess.
You are allowed to feel.
You are allowed to break.
You are allowed to heal.

It's okay to not be okay.
Just don't stop moving forward.
You'll find your way—piece by piece.

And when you feel like you didn't deserve all this pain, all this chaos—pause. Breathe. Because you didn't. And you should know this: at the end of the day, *you matter*. You deserve peace. You deserve love.
You deserve to heal.

"The Weight We Hide"

Have you ever noticed how some days you wake up feeling light, and other days it's like you're drowning in thoughts before you even open your eyes? It's not that the pain is gone—it's just that for a moment, you forgot it. You buried it deep enough to breathe for a while. But that doesn't mean you're okay.

I know you're carrying a lot. You smile like it's easy, like nothing ever happened. But I see it—the tired eyes, the quiet sighs, the way you zone out when the room gets too loud. You can fake it for a day. Maybe two. Maybe even a week. But how long can you keep hiding from what's really inside you?

Eventually, it spills. One word, one glance, one unexpected moment—and you break. And that's not weakness, it's truth trying to find a way out.

You're carrying so much weight, but hiding it only adds more. It's like dragging a heavy bag and pretending it's empty. You don't have to do that. If someone hurt you, say it. If their words cut deep, don't just laugh it off and act like it didn't touch you. Because I know you—you're not the type to fake care, so don't let yourself start faking peace either.

Lately, I've seen you building a fake world around you. Smiling when it hurts. Nodding when you want to scream. Pretending things are fine when they're clearly not. And yeah, maybe people don't always deserve to hear your side. But **you** deserve to *feel* your side. You deserve to be honest with yourself.

Maybe it's time to talk to someone—*really* talk. Someone trustworthy. I know that's not easy right now. You don't trust easily anymore, and deep down, you're scared that opening up will just go wrong again. I get that. Honestly? You're not wrong. From experience, I can tell you—sometimes a third person can walk into a friendship, or a relationship, and ruin everything. And it's only afterward that you realize… none of it was your fault. It was never about you.

That's why my biggest advice? Write it down. Pour yourself into a book. An empty room might have ears, but an empty page never will.

If there's someone you still think about—try. Talk to them once. Maybe twice. But not more than three times. If they wanted to understand you, they would. If they wanted you, they'd show up. You don't owe anyone endless versions of yourself just to be heard. Speak when it helps. But if it starts to hurt, stay quiet. Watch. Protect your peace.

Have you ever noticed that when *you* stop putting in effort, the friendship just fades? Like you were the only one watering a dead plant, hoping it'd grow. At some point, you've got to stop waiting. Stop reaching. Stop breaking your own heart by holding onto people who already let go.

And maybe the hardest truth? The world keeps turning without you. People go on. They smile. They laugh. They live. And sometimes, it hits you—the people you taught how to feel normal are okay now… and you're the one who feels missing. You realize, when you disappear, not everyone comes looking. And that stings.

But that doesn't make *you* any less. That just shows who was really there, and who was only there for the parts of you that made their life easier.

Honestly, if you feel like walking away—*do it*. Not to prove a point. Not to be dramatic. But to finally give yourself the space to reflect. To breathe. To understand where everything started to fall apart.

Look back—just a year ago, everything was different. One year can change *so much* in a person. You've grown. You've broken. You've rebuilt. And through it all, you've been carrying a weight that was never fully yours to begin with.

Walking away is *not* selfish. What slowly breaks you is holding on to people who were never planning to come back. Whether it's friends, family, or someone you loved—if they constantly make you feel small, unseen, or not enough, you don't have to stay. You don't have to keep waiting for the day they'll finally value you. Because maybe… they never will.

Sometimes, you do everything with the purest heart—and still, you're called selfish. Or dramatic. Or "too sensitive." Blah, blah, blah. But hey—**wake up**. Just because they said something about you doesn't mean it's *true*. Don't start believing the version of you that lives in their heads. That's not who you are.

You've got your own life to build. Your dreams to chase. Your future to step into. You don't have time to sit around overthinking what they said, or burying it deep inside you like it's your truth. It's *not*. And honestly? This thing you're going through—it feels heavy, yes. But it's not the end of the world.

There are real problems out there—poverty, war, pain we can't even imagine. And while what you're feeling matters, this is still just *a page* in your book. Just a chapter. Not the whole story.

Your life? It's like a book with a million chapters. Some are painful. Some are messy. Some are heartwarming. And some will completely change you. But if you don't turn the page, you'll never know what's next. You'll stay stuck in the same paragraph, reading the same pain over and over again.

And you know what happens if you just keep bottling it all up? If you keep pretending it's nothing, keep hiding it under that fake smile? *Nothing* will get better. You'll end up stuck in another cycle of sadness, another round of silence, another version of depression that looks just like the last.

So don't let that happen. You're allowed to feel. You're allowed to be hurt. But you're also allowed to walk away. To rest. To reflect. And most of all—**to move on.**

People may drift, change, or ignore you. You may feel replaced, or the bonds may just break. The person who felt like home yesterday now feels so hard to reach, and if you know, you know.

Face Your Hurt

It's essential to acknowledge the pain you're carrying, even when it feels like no one sees or understands it. Hurt is something we all experience, yet we're often taught to suppress it, dismiss it, or deny it altogether. Whether it's a harsh word from someone close, a betrayal from a friend, or just that overwhelming emptiness inside, we all face moments where we feel broken.

Here's the truth: most people never truly admit their pain. And even when they do, they often struggle to pinpoint the cause or the person behind it.

The hardest part of healing is realizing that sometimes, we are the ones holding onto the hurt. We let it linger inside, pretending everything is fine, carrying it around like an invisible burden. But it's okay to not be okay. It's okay to feel broken, to feel weighed down by a pain you can't seem to shake off. The first step is acknowledging that hurt—stopping the pretense that it doesn't exist.

I know it's not easy. I know you care deeply about those who may have hurt you—family, friends, even strangers who have left scars in their wake. But my dear, you owe it to yourself to finally face that pain. It's time to feel it, to sit with it, and realize that feeling hurt is not a weakness—it's part of the healing process.

When you allow yourself to truly feel, you'll start to see the sources of your pain. You'll recognize the people and situations that drain you, that chip away at your self-worth, and steal your joy. This awareness is key. It's not just about identifying the ones who hurt you, but understanding why you allowed them that power over you for so long.

You don't have to keep holding onto relationships or situations that only bring you pain. Sometimes, the hardest choice is to distance yourself from those who don't nurture your peace. It's a difficult decision, especially when you care about them, but remember: you can't pour from an empty cup. You can't keep giving love to those who drain your spirit.

Now is the time to set boundaries, to create space for your own healing. You deserve peace, and that means sometimes choosing yourself first. It's time to reclaim your energy—mentally, emotionally, and spiritually. And as you grow stronger, you'll realize that not everyone is meant to stay in your life. Those who truly care will respect your boundaries, support your healing, and bring you peace—not chaos.

You don't have to carry this burden anymore. Let it go. Feel the hurt, embrace it, learn from it, and step into a life where self-love and strength guide you. You are worthy of healing. You are worthy of happiness. You deserve a life where peace and joy are your constant companions.

In the silence of your pain,
 When the world feels far away,
 Let the hurt rise like the rain,
 And wash your doubts away.

Feel the sting, let it breathe,
For it's part of who you are.
You can't heal if you don't grieve,
And you've been living with that scar.

Let go of the weight you carry,
And the people who don't care.
You deserve a heart that's merry,
Not one left in despair.

So embrace your hurt, don't run,
Let it teach you how to heal.
You're stronger now, you've won—
In your pain, you'll find what's real.

*The deepest wounds are often the ones we hide the longest.
But when you face them, you discover a strength you never
knew you had.*

Scars That Speak

Some wounds just become scars we wish we could erase. On normal days, we walk around like everything's fine. We don't even realize we're pretending — until the quiet comes. When we're alone, it starts to haunt us. The pain seeps in, making us doubt ourselves. We remember the nights we cried silently, the moments we reacted in ways even we didn't understand, the countless times we felt fed up with the world around us.

Now, all we try to do is make peace — to accept people the way they are. But deep inside, it feels impossible.
Because the truth is, some scars are made when bonds break. We crave the old connections, the comfort of people who once felt like home. We long for that one person to stay, to fight for us. But sometimes, they move on like nothing ever happened. They don't notice the gap they left behind.

Bruh, trust me — if someone moves on without a second thought, if they don't even feel the difference your absence makes, there's no use holding on.
You were never their priority. Maybe you never will be.

It hurts, I know. It feels like you're being replaced, forgotten. But hear me — good things take time. The right people, the ones who'll make you their priority, they exist. And they're worth the wait. Someone will give you the love you deserve, the happiness you've always wished for.

Now, stop reading for a moment.
Breathe. Reflect.

What hurts you the most — is it them, or what they said?
 Did they really mean to hurt you? Or were they just lost in
their own anger?

Think about it.
 Did you deserve the way they treated you?
 Nah.
 No one deserves that. Not you. Not anyone.

After reading this, I want you to do one thing.
 Go to your favorite spot — maybe it's a quiet corner, under a
tree, standing in front of your mirror, or simply anywhere you
feel safe. Talk to yourself.
 Speak it all out.
 Give yourself the advice you wish someone else would have
given you. Be your own therapist.
 If you have anger buried deep inside, pour it out. Cry if you
have to. Yell if you need to. Whisper if that's all you can
manage. But let it out. Don't carry it alone anymore.

I know — sometimes it feels like it's too much.
 The feeling of wanting to give up, to disappear, it sneaks in
like a storm.
 But listen to me: Are you insane to believe that your absence
will somehow fix the world around you?
 That's foolish, my love.
 Understand this — if your presence doesn't affect certain
people, neither will your absence.
 But does that mean your life has no value? Never.

There's no guarantee that the people you have today will be
there tomorrow.
 And that's okay.
 Because your life isn't meant to be lived for *just one person*.
 You meet millions of people in this lifetime. One bad

experience, one broken bond — it doesn't define the nine lakh ninety-nine thousand nine hundred and ninety-nine other souls still waiting to meet your magic.

There are people like you out there.
 And for me?
 You exist.
 You matter.

I know you will feel like removing these scars isn't easy. You might read this and think that what I'm saying is just a temporary way to make you feel better. Or maybe you're wondering, "What do you know about the pain I'm going through?" And honestly, I get it. I can't pretend to understand your exact struggles, but I do understand pain. I understand feeling lost and broken. But, just for a moment, stop and ask yourself—*is it worth it?* Is holding onto the hurt, the anger, the betrayal really worth it? They've been cruel, they've made you feel small, and yet, through all that, you stayed silent. You didn't retaliate, you didn't let it consume you. And that right there? That makes you the bigger person. That makes you stronger than they could ever understand.

Look at what you've been carrying—the weight of all the hurt they've thrown your way. It feels impossible to hold sometimes, doesn't it? But here you are. You are still standing. You've felt the deepest pain, and yet, you're still here. The weight you've carried has shaped you into someone that even you might not fully recognize yet. You've been through hell, but the fire didn't burn you, it *forged* you. Every tear, every sleepless night, every single moment where you thought you couldn't go on... they've all added to this strength that you now have within you. You are stronger than you think, stronger than you've ever known.

They hurt you, and you didn't deserve any of it. You didn't
ask for the heartache. You didn't deserve to feel abandoned,
neglected, or unimportant. But despite everything, you're still
breathing. You're still fighting. And that? That makes you one
of the strongest people I know. The scars you carry? They're
not just reminders of pain; they're proof of your survival.
Proof that you didn't let the darkness swallow you. You are
here. And you have every right to be proud of that.

You see, each scar tells a story. A story of someone who's
been knocked down and still got back up. A story of someone
who's been betrayed, hurt, and misunderstood, yet chose to
keep going. You've walked through storms, and you've come
out the other side. And those storms? They didn't break you.
They made you *stronger*.

So don't you dare think for a second that your struggles have
been in vain. Those battles you fought on your own? They've
shaped you into a version of yourself that is unstoppable.
Even when you felt like giving up, you pushed through.
You've become someone who is not only resilient but
beautiful in the strength you've gained. You are no longer just
a survivor—you are a warrior.

And trust me when I say this: you are more than enough. You
have always been enough. And even if it feels like you've lost
everything, remember that this pain is only temporary. It
might feel like forever, but it won't last. The scars will fade,
the heart will heal, and you'll emerge stronger, more
powerful, and more at peace than you ever thought possible

Okay, I know you know exactly what hurt you the most. And
now, it's time to face it. It's time to confront that pain head-on,
to no longer let it control you. It's time to stop pretending like
it doesn't matter, like you're fine when you're not. Speak up

for yourself. Stand tall. Because you've spent way too long letting them treat you however they want. But no more. You are not their punching bag, their emotional outlet, or their doormat. You are your own person, and it's time you start acting like it.

Stop hiding behind the walls you've built to protect yourself. I get it, it's scary. The fear of rejection, the fear of being misunderstood, it's real. But listen to me—*you deserve respect*. You deserve to be heard. You don't need to continue being their silent witness to their cruelty or indifference. You have every right to express your pain, your frustration, your anger. And if they can't handle it? That's on them.

You've been through so much, carried so many burdens, and it's time to stop carrying the weight of their actions, their words, their treatment of you. It's time to put yourself first for once. Time to stop allowing them to take advantage of your kindness, your patience, your understanding. You owe yourself that. You owe yourself the peace of mind that comes with knowing you've stood up for what's right—for yourself.

Speak your truth, no matter how hard it is. It's not about hurting them back; it's about showing them that you have a voice, and you're not afraid to use it. It's about showing yourself that you're strong enough to walk away from what hurts you, and step into a place where you can heal, grow, and finally breathe again.

So stand up. Face it. Face them. And remind yourself that your worth isn't defined by how they treat you. Your worth is intrinsic, it's unshakeable, and it's time you started believing in it, as fiercely as you've believed in others.

Revenge Lowers You

After reading all these pages, you begin to understand that what they did to you was wrong. And now, a feeling stirs within you—a desire for revenge. You want them to feel the same pain, the same bullshit that you went through. You want them to experience what it felt like when they broke you. The anger and frustration bubble up inside, and it's hard to ignore the urge to make them pay for the hurt they caused.

But my love, that's not how life works. You have so much more ahead of you, and revenge isn't worth the energy it takes to feed that fire. It's easy to think that hurting them will somehow make everything right, but in reality, it won't. It's best to go silent, step back, and heal yourself first.

Healing isn't about getting back at someone; it's about finding peace and reclaiming your own strength. The world doesn't need you to carry the weight of their wrongs.

Now, let's say you get your revenge. You hurt the person who hurt you. For a moment, it might feel sweet—there's satisfaction, there's a brief sense of victory, as if everything is now balanced. It might feel like justice, like you've finally gotten back what was taken from you. But here's the truth—after that moment, the guilt will hit you like a wave crashing over everything.

You'll wonder if it was worth it. You'll question if you truly wanted to become someone who hurt others to make themselves feel better. The weight of it will start to sink in, and you'll realize that it didn't change anything, except perhaps, make you feel more lost.

And here's the bigger question—seeking revenge doesn't change anything. It doesn't make you feel better in the long run. It doesn't undo the pain. If you seek revenge, what will be the difference between you and the person who hurt you? Wouldn't you become the bad person too? In the end, we all have a choice: to rise above, or to let ourselves be dragged into the same cycle of hurt and bitterness.

It's time to let go, my love. It's time to move forward and find your peace. Revenge only keeps you tied to the past, but healing? Healing sets you free.

Revenge is not everything. It might seem like the only way to ease your pain, to make things right again, but deep down, you know it's not the answer. You have so much more to offer, so many dreams and aspirations that are waiting for you. Why waste your energy on someone who doesn't even deserve a second thought in your life?

There's a whole world out there for you to explore, experiences to be lived, people to meet, and passions to pursue. Why would you let someone's hurtful actions trap you in a cycle of bitterness and anger? Life is too precious, too short, to waste on revenge. You have better things to do with your time. You have your own growth to focus on, your own happiness to chase. Your future holds more than the pain of the past.

Think about what you could achieve if you channeled that energy into something positive—into the things that truly matter. Your talents, your dreams, your love for life—those are the things that will bring you fulfillment. Revenge will only leave you stuck in the past, but pursuing your own happiness will set you free.

Remember, your worth isn't defined by how others treat you. It's defined by how you choose to rise above the hurt and move forward. Don't let the actions of one person take away your future. You are capable of so much more than revenge—you are capable of healing, growth, and building the life you deserve. So don't waste another moment thinking about what they did to you. Focus on what you can do for yourself, and trust that in time, everything else will fall into place.

Revenge may seem like justice, but real justice is living your life on your own terms, free from the burden of the past. You've already shown your strength by surviving the hurt. Now it's time to show even greater strength by moving forward. And trust me, that's where your true power lies.

At the end of the day, you're a much better person than to make someone go through what they did to you. Holding onto the desire for revenge only keeps you tied to the pain of the past. It's easy to get caught up in the idea that the only way to heal is to make them feel the same hurt. But that's not who you are, and that's not the path you want to walk.

So, remember this: You're better than that. You are better than anyone who tries to bring you down, better than the hurt they caused, and better than any urge for vengeance. Your journey is about growth, healing, and becoming the person you're meant to be. And none of that includes dragging someone else down to the depths of your pain.

You're already winning by choosing to rise above it. And that's where your true strength lies

Speaking Up Is Not Revenge

Okay, I know exactly what you're feeling right now. You're standing at a crossroads, trembling between two fires — speaking up or seeking revenge. Your heart is tired, confused, heavy with all the pain you never asked for. And a small, broken part of you wonders if speaking your truth might make you look like the bad one too.

But hear me loud and clear — you didn't deserve any of this. You didn't ask to be broken, you didn't invite the betrayal, and you certainly didn't deserve the way they treated you like you didn't matter. You were just trying to love, to trust, to be there. And if you didn't deserve that hurt, then you don't deserve to carry its burden on your shoulders anymore. It's not yours to carry. Not anymore.

Speaking up is not revenge. Speaking up is not anger. Speaking up is standing in front of your own reflection and whispering, "I deserved better." Speaking up is not about making them hurt the way they hurt you — because let's be real — some people can never feel what they make others go through. Speaking up is about reclaiming what they tried to shatter — your worth, your dignity, your voice.

You might wonder if they will ever understand the depth of the scar they left behind. Let me tell you — if they had cared, they would have noticed the first time your smile faded. The first time your laughter died in your throat. They would have felt the cold in your silence, the hurt in your distance. If they didn't, they probably never will. And the brutal truth? You don't owe them an explanation for your wounds.

All you ever need to say — to them, or maybe just to yourself — is, "What you did hurt me. It broke pieces of me I didn't even know could break. And I will not let it happen again." That's enough. That's more than enough. Because it's no longer about them anymore. It's about *you*. It's about your healing. Your peace. Your future.

Don't fall into the trap of thinking silence will make them realize your worth. Don't stay quiet hoping they'll wake up one day full of guilt and regret. If they didn't value you when you gave them everything, why would they mourn you when you walk away silently? Your heart has already spent too long waiting for an apology, for closure, for something that might never come.
 And you deserve more than waiting. You deserve more than silent prayers and tear-stained pillows.

Speaking up isn't cruelty. It's an act of courage. It's choosing to stand tall even when every bone in your body feels shattered. It's looking pain in the eye and saying, "You will not define me." Even when it hurts. Even when it feels easier to disappear into the background.

Because if you fall into the spiral of revenge, if you keep replaying their betrayal and trying to match their cruelty, you will only keep slicing yourself open for people who will never bleed for you.
 You'll stay trapped — in anger, in sadness, in an endless, exhausting loop that drains the very soul out of you.

And you? You are meant for more than that. You are meant to be free.

If you hold onto what they did, if you keep watering the hurt they caused, it will only grow roots deeper into your heart. They will continue to exist inside you, haunting your peace,

poisoning your joy.
 But if you let go — if you truly, finally let go — they lose their power. They lose their place in your heart, in your mind, in your story.

So here's where you stand.
 You have two choices:

You can speak up — look them in the eye and tell them their actions tore you apart — and then walk away with your head held high.
 Or you can stay silent — deny them even the satisfaction of your words — and erase them from your existence like they never even deserved a chapter in your story.

Either way, my love, you move on.
 You move forward, carrying nothing but your strength, your wisdom, your resilience.
 You leave behind the bitterness, the unanswered questions, the hope that maybe they would someday be better.

Because staying — waiting — hoping — that will only chain you to a heartbreak that should have never been yours to bear.

Speaking up tells yourself, *"I matter too much to be hurt in silence."*
 Ignoring them tells yourself, *"My peace matters more than their apology."*

But no matter which road you choose — whether you walk away in roaring thunder or silent grace — remember: the endgame is not revenge. It's not even closure from them.

The ultimate goal is freedom.
 The ultimate goal is peace.
 The ultimate goal is moving on.

And you will, my beautiful warrior.
You absolutely will.
You already are

And at the end of the day, it's your kindness, your goodness, your heart — that's what truly matters.
It's not about what they did. It's not about how they failed you, or how they made you question your worth. Their actions don't define you. Your response does. The love you still carry inside, the gentleness you refuse to let go of — that's who you are. And no one can take that away from you.

It's the fact that you chose to remain gentle in a world that tried every way possible to harden you.
A world that pushed you, hurt you, broke you — yet you didn't let it turn you into someone bitter. You didn't let it rob you of your softness. You still smile. You still care. You still hope. And that strength? That's rare. That's beautiful. That's powerful.

It's the fact that you chose to heal instead of hate.
You could have carried the anger. You could have mirrored their cruelty. You could have shut your heart and built walls so high that no one could ever touch you again. But you didn't. You chose to feel every ache, every crack, and still mend yourself with love, patience, and grace.
You chose healing. You chose you.

It's the fact that even after everything — after all the times you were left wondering why you weren't enough — you still believe in love, you still believe in hope, and most of all, you still believe in yourself.
That belief, that spark inside you, it's unbreakable. They couldn't dim it. They couldn't steal it. It's yours, burning quietly, steadily, lighting up your path forward.

And that, my love — that is your real victory.
 Not their regret. Not their apology.
 Your real victory is the way you kept your soul intact.
 Your real victory is the way you became even more yourself,
even after everything.

Karma Speaks

You know, sometimes it's easy to wonder, *"How will the person who hurt me ever realize what they did was wrong?"* But here's the thing — that's what karma is for. You don't need to seek revenge, because karma will take care of it. What goes around, truly does come back around. The most important part is that you didn't allow yourself to sink to their level; you chose not to react in anger or hate. And that is what truly matters in the grand scheme of things.

Let's be practical for a moment. Imagine, at the end of the day, when you meet God, He won't ask you, *"Why did you do what you did?"* Instead, He'll say, *"What you did was wrong."* The focus is never on why you acted the way you did — it's about whether your actions were right. In the end, it's not about what others did to you, but about how you responded. It's not about the wrongs done to you; it's about the good you chose to do, regardless of the circumstances.

At the end of the day, it's always between you and karma. The choices you make, the kindness you show, and the good deeds you perform matter more than any wrong done to you. You carry those actions with you, and they shape the future in ways that revenge never will. So, while others may act badly, you have the power to stay true to your path. Karma will always find its way, but it's your goodness that defines who you are.

Be a Good Person, Not a People Pleaser

Every time you say "yes" when you really mean "no," you pull a piece out of yourself. Every time you prioritize someone else's comfort over your own, you lose another part of who you are. Every time you hold back your feelings to avoid upsetting someone, another piece fades away.

At first, nothing seems to change. The tower still stands, and you tell yourself, *"I can handle this."* But with every piece you give away, you become less of yourself. Until one day, someone asks for just one more thing — something small, something you should easily be able to do. But this time, you break. Not because of that one request, but because of everything you've already given away before it.

People-pleasing doesn't make you more loved — it makes you less whole. You can give, but don't give so much that there's nothing left for you

It's time you understand that being a good person actually starts with being good to yourself. Often, you stop yourself from saying or doing things because you're worried it might hurt someone else. And yes, you're already a good person for that. But here's the truth: don't keep putting others ahead of yourself, don't prioritize their comfort at the cost of your own well-being. Because, at the end of the day, it's you who ends up overthinking, crying, and carrying the weight, while the other person sleeps peacefully, unaffected.

It's time to recognize that you, too, matter. Karma is real, and your kindness doesn't go unnoticed. Your goodness has the power to influence the people around you, making them kinder, more compassionate, and more understanding. But remember, it's also time to let go. Let go of the things and situations that constantly pull you down and cause you mental breakdowns. Don't carry the burden of others' actions or expectations.

My love, trust in karma — let it do the honors. You don't need to fix everything or everyone. Life has its own way of returning what you give, and sometimes, the best thing you can do is step back and let things unfold as they should. Karma is real, and it has a way of balancing everything.

It's time to move on. What they did to you was wrong, and you didn't deserve any of it. But the real strength lies not in seeking revenge or holding onto bitterness, but in choosing to rise above it. You've already endured the hurt, and now it's time to release it. Holding on to anger or pain doesn't make you stronger — it only keeps you trapped in a cycle that prevents you from growing. Be the mature person who understands that while their actions were wrong, you don't need to repeat the same mistakes. Let go of the weight of their actions, and move forward with peace in your heart. You don't need to prove anything to them; your true power is in moving on, healing, and finding your peace, regardless of what they did. Life is too short to stay anchored in the past. It's your time to live free.

By choosing to let go, you don't just free yourself from the hurt, you create space for new beginnings. And that's where true healing starts — not from revenge, but from the decision to move forward and let karma handle the rest.

Understand the Hurt

Sometimes, when we are hurt, we don't even know why it hurts so much. It's because it's hard to accept that the person who hurt us mattered the most. Accepting that someone had that much importance in our lives feels painful.

At this point, we start believing that *we* are the bad ones. That maybe something is wrong with us. Social media makes this even worse — especially Instagram. If you're sad, it shows you more sadness. If you're doubting yourself, it pushes you deeper into that hole. Without even realizing it, we let our mind spiral into more pain.

But here's the truth: we are not even trying to understand what is actually hurting us. It's like someone cuts your finger, and instead of treating the cut, you keep stabbing it deeper, asking yourself why it happened, thinking you deserve the pain.

Isn't that complete nonsense?

We need to relate this to real life, to real emotional situations. The pain doesn't mean you are a bad person. The pain simply means — you cared.

In life, hurt is often seen when expectations break, especially by the people we love the most. Sometimes, it's not even the actions that hurt us the most, but the words they say. Words that linger and echo. Throwing a stone into the ocean is easy, but stop and wonder — how deep did that stone really go? That's how some words feel. They sink deep into your heart, far beyond what anyone can see.

I know it's really hard to accept the hurt because, deep down, it feels like admitting that you are giving up on them. Somewhere in your heart, there's still a whisper — "Maybe if I try once more, things will go back to normal." But trust me, you've already tried so many times. You can never change the other person, but you can change yourself. You can only protect your own heart.

Accepting the pain feels terrifying because it means admitting that someone had the power to affect you, to hurt you. We fear that if we accept it, it will consume us. But that's the lie we tell ourselves. Resisting the pain only makes it worse. Healing doesn't come from fighting the hurt — it comes from understanding it, feeling it, and allowing yourself to move forward.

Once you start accepting the pain, it no longer holds as much power over you. It doesn't mean the hurt will disappear overnight. It means that, slowly, you will learn to live with it, to let it coexist without letting it define you. You will realize that it's okay to feel broken. It's okay to feel like everything is falling apart. Sometimes, we have to break in order to rebuild.

You don't have to have all the answers right away. You don't need to know *why* the hurt happened. You only need to acknowledge that it did. And that, *in itself*, is enough. The truth is, healing is not linear. There will be days when you feel like you've moved on, and then something will trigger that pain again. But that's okay. Every time you face it, every time you accept it, you get a little stronger.

The people who hurt you, they don't define your worth. Your worth was never tied to how others treated you. Your value is in how you treat yourself — with kindness, with patience, and with the strength to rise above.

Healing isn't about erasing the past. It's about learning to carry it, to grow with it, and to transform the pain into something powerful. Every scar you have is a reminder that you survived, that you faced the hurt and chose to move forward.

So take your time. Don't rush the process. You are not broken beyond repair. You are just in the middle of something beautiful — a journey of becoming the strongest version of yourself.

See, that's the first step — you understand *why* it hurts you and *what* hurts you. It's only then that you begin to learn how to live with it. And I'll give you an example to help you visualize this better:

Take a candle. Now, stab it with a lot of iron nails, and light the candle. Watch the wax melt. You'll see that the nails remain stuck in the wax, and the wax, despite all the damage, keeps flowing around them.

What's happening here? You're not trying to pull the nails out or running away from them. No, you're learning to live with the nails inside. The candle keeps burning, and the wax continues to melt, but the nails are now part of it. The pain is not something you push away. It becomes something you carry with you, yet still continue to move forward.

In the same way, your body and soul need to learn how to coexist with the pain, how to live with it without letting it define you. You don't need to *fix* everything all at once. You don't need to force the nails out. Sometimes, the healing comes in simply allowing yourself to exist with the hurt, knowing that the light of who you are can still shine despite the weight you carry.

Learning to live with the pain isn't about ignoring it or pretending it's not there. It's about giving yourself permission to feel the hurt, without letting it control you. Think of it like the candle. The nails don't disappear, but the wax keeps melting, it keeps flowing. That's the key. You *flow* through life, despite the pain you carry.

Over time, the nails may start to feel less sharp. The pain might not sting as much, but it will always be there, just like the nails are in the wax. And that's okay. Pain is a part of life. It's part of what makes us human. The more you accept that, the more you'll realize that it doesn't have to stop you from living fully.

It's easy to get stuck in the "why" — why did this happen, why did they hurt me, why me? But the truth is, sometimes there is no answer. Sometimes, there is no reason that will make the pain easier to bear. So instead of asking "why," ask yourself, "What now?" What will you do with the pain? How will you use it to grow?

Just like the candle, you don't need to get rid of the pain to keep shining. You can keep burning with that light, even if there are scars. Those scars, those nails, become part of your story. They are a testament to your strength, to your ability to continue, to keep living despite what's been done to you.

Healing doesn't happen all at once. It's not a linear path. One day, you might feel fine, and the next day, the pain might come rushing back. And that's okay. The process is messy, and it takes time. Be patient with yourself. Let yourself *feel* everything, but don't let it stop you. You are allowed to heal at your own pace.

And as you learn to live with the pain, you'll discover that it's not as powerful as you once thought. It doesn't control you.

You control how you respond to it. You are still whole, even with the cracks.

It hit me hard when I realized how things change.

When priorities shift,
Replies become delayed,
Conversations start to fade,
And sometimes, situations are blamed—
Or even worse, you're blamed.
People say you've changed,
And everyone might think you're rude or selfish,
But that's not who you really are. You know your heart.
You tried your best, always with good intentions,
But somewhere along the way,
You forgot to be good to yourself.

Did you ever stop and think about all the energy you poured into that one friendship, or into that one person? You nearly lost yourself in the process.
You blamed yourself for things you never even did.
Now, you're emotionally drained.
But listen, you have to stay true to who you are. It's time to move on.
For your own sake, **just move on.**

Let It Go

Sometimes, it's better to let go. You have to allow people to leave your life without chasing after them. Often, people only realize your value when you stop giving them all your care, attention, and energy. They begin to crave the love and effort they once took for granted. Letting go isn't about anger or bitterness — it's about choosing yourself. It's about protecting your emotional well-being and finding peace within yourself. Holding on too tightly to people who don't appreciate you only drains your spirit. Sometimes, the best thing you can do for yourself is to move forward and let them realize what they lost on their own.

Learn to grow up. One fight, one hurtful moment doesn't deserve to take away your mental peace. It's time to allow new people to enter your life and let others move on. That's life — people come, people leave, and you have to accept it. Understand the change. Be the mature one.

Let me give you an example. Imagine you have a shirt with a broken button. What do you do? You fix the button and continue wearing the shirt — you don't throw the entire shirt away because of one small tear. In the same way, think of a plant that refuses to grow. You don't get angry at the plant. Instead, you change its environment — you move it somewhere it can breathe better, grow stronger. Life demands the same kind of patience and understanding.

Sometimes, you and the people you once held close simply grow apart. Life pulls you in different directions — responsibilities pile up, priorities shift, and without realizing it, you both become passengers on separate journeys. It's no one's fault. It's just life moving forward. And sometimes, holding on too tightly only causes more pain.

Letting go doesn't mean you didn't care; it means you care enough about yourself to protect your own peace. It means you respect the memories, but you also respect the person you are becoming. Moving on is not about erasing the past — it's about understanding that not everyone is meant to stay till the end. Some people are just chapters, not the whole story. And that's okay. Let them go with gratitude, not anger, because every bond, even the broken ones, taught you something valuable.

Take a clean, fresh sheet of paper. Now imagine crumbling a part of it for every bad incident — every harsh word, every silent night, every broken promise. Afterward, even if you try to smooth it back out, no matter how many times you say sorry, the paper will never look the same.

That's what happens with some bonds. No matter how hard you try, some connections never return to how they once were. And you, my love, need to understand that. You need to let it go — for your heart, for your soul, and for the beautiful future waiting for you.

Now, let me shift your perspective.

Ask yourself — if you stop texting first, if you stop making plans, if you stop walking up to them... will they ever come to you? Deep down, you already know the answer. If your presence truly mattered, you wouldn't have to keep chasing it. The sad truth is, without you, it probably won't affect them at all. Not even a little.

So move on. Let them leave. Let people go.

But whatever happens, don't lose yourself in the process. Don't let that pure, kind-hearted inner child inside you fade away. Protect it. Cherish it. Love it — because that part of you is rare, and it deserves to stay alive no matter who stays or who leaves.

One day, I asked myself — *Smina, if you go offline for a day, does it really affect anyone?* No. If you stay in bed for weeks, completely drained and exhausted, does it change anything for anyone? No. The people who made you feel ignored, the ones who hurt you — they will continue living their lives like nothing ever happened.
 And that's when it hit me — the only people who would truly notice your silence, who would genuinely worry about your tears, are your parents. They are the ones who will never leave your side.
 So tell me — is all this drama, all this pain over temporary people, really necessary? Can't you just let it go and hold on to the ones who actually care?

Yeah — that's the hard reality. And you should accept it.

If you know your plane is going to crash, would you still board it just because you already bought the ticket?
 No. You would save yourself.
 In the same way, just because you invested time, energy, and love into someone doesn't mean you have to stay and crash with them. Your peace is more important than your past investments.
 Save yourself. Choose yourself. Let it go.

Do you understand the strength that comes with letting go? It's not about forgetting or excusing what happened; it's about accepting the reality of the situation and choosing to move forward. Letting go means you forgive not to repair the broken bond but to release yourself from the weight of resentment. You forgive to bring peace to your heart, not because they necessarily deserve it, but because *you* deserve the freedom. It's a conscious decision to stop investing your time, emotions, and energy into something that no longer serves you. When you let go, you free yourself from the need to change the past and stop holding on to what's beyond your control. You choose to live in the present, unburdened, and empowered, knowing that sometimes walking away is the best thing you can do for yourself.

Ultimately, letting go isn't just about others; it's about *you* — your peace, your happiness, your growth. It's an act of self-care, not weakness. When you release what no longer fits your life, you make space for the things and people that truly align with who you are becoming. And in that freedom, you'll find the strength to move forward, embracing each new chapter with an open heart and mind.

Letting go isn't just about releasing someone, it's about freeing yourself from the weight of what they left behind. It's realizing that holding onto the past, the hurt, the questions, the 'what-ifs' — all of it keeps you from moving forward. Letting go isn't an easy choice. It's an act of courage, where you decide to choose your own peace over the chaos that someone else's actions created. It's in those quiet moments when you stop chasing after what isn't meant for you, that you discover the power of your own heart — a heart that is strong enough to love itself first. And when you do that, you realize you're no longer bound to them, or to the person you thought they were. You are free to walk away, to rebuild, to breathe, to become something more than the person you were when you were waiting. You don't need anyone's validation to know you're worthy — sometimes, it's about knowing that letting go is the only way to find yourself again.

Move On

It's time to move on — from that one situation, from that one incident. If you think back, you'll realize how after that moment, everything slowly started falling apart. It's not just you who feels this way. It's like that one event flipped a switch, and suddenly people around you began showing their true colors. And honestly, what was your fault in any of it? Sometimes, no matter how pure your intentions were, people still choose to misunderstand you, hurt you, or leave you. That's exactly why you have to move on. Staying stuck in that pain only holds you back from everything beautiful that's still waiting for you. Moving on isn't about forgetting — it's about choosing yourself over the chaos they left behind.

Now you know what they did to you.
 And honestly, I blame you — because you let them.
 You gave them the power to hurt you, and they used it without a second thought.
 It's almost funny, isn't it? You kept reaching out for the rose, knowing it would prick you with its thorns, yet you stayed — hoping, bleeding, waiting.
 When all along, there were millions of sunflowers blooming around you — open, warm, and waiting to love you without asking you to bleed first. You spent so long staring at the thorns that you missed the entire field of sunflowers blooming around you. And don't you think it's finally time to move on? You've already taken the first step by letting them go — now the real work is about forgiving them and, even more importantly, forgiving yourself. Not for being too trusting. Not for being too kind. But for believing that they would treat your heart the way you treated theirs.

Forgiving doesn't mean forgetting. It doesn't mean wiping the slate clean and acting like nothing ever happened. If you try to forget everything, you risk falling back into that endless cycle of pain — the one where you keep hoping for change that will never come. Remembering is important. Remember what hurt you so you don't touch the same fire twice. Remember what lessons it taught you, but don't carry the bitterness. Carry the wisdom. Carry the strength.

You forgive not because they deserve your forgiveness, but because you deserve peace. You forgive to set yourself free from the heaviness you were never meant to hold. You forgive so you can breathe without aching, so you can laugh without guilt, so you can love yourself harder than anyone ever could. Forgiveness is not about making excuses for them. It's about making space for yourself to heal, grow, and live without dragging the chains of old pain behind you.

You are not meant to stay trapped in the same heartbreak, replaying the same memories over and over. You are meant to rise above it. You are meant to heal so deeply that the memory no longer stings, it just becomes a story — a chapter you once read, not a prison you still live in. Moving on isn't about weakness. It's about realizing that your heart deserves better. It's about believing that there is so much more waiting for you ahead than anything you're leaving behind.

You forgive them because you are a good human, because your heart is kind even when it has every reason not to be. And I know—it's not easy. It takes everything in you to let go of the hurt, to release the weight of what they did, to stop replaying the "what-ifs" in your mind. But if you never take the first step toward moving on, you never truly will. You'll stay stuck in the same place, carrying the same pain, while life moves forward without you.

Trust me, moving on becomes easier once you do it. The first time feels impossible, like tearing yourself away from something that was once a part of you. But once you learn how to let go, it becomes a habit—a habit of choosing yourself, of protecting your peace, of walking away from what no longer serves you. And like any habit, it takes time. It takes patience. But one day, you'll wake up and realize that the pain doesn't sting the same way anymore. You'll breathe lighter. You'll laugh freely. You'll see that moving on wasn't just about forgetting them—it was about remembering *you.*

Okay, dummy — stop creating fake scenarios in your head. Stop imagining that one day they'll come back, pleading for you, realizing your worth. Once you decide to move on, there's no reason to keep looking back. You don't read your books backwards, right? Life is the same. It moves forward, not in reverse. My love, that's just how life works — and the sooner you accept it, the easier it becomes to breathe again. Learn. Accept. Move on.

Some people come into your life only to bring chaos, to teach you lessons the hard way. And you? You move on because you learned yours. You don't stay stuck. You don't sit there picking up the broken pieces hoping they'll magically become whole again. No. You honor the lesson, but you honor yourself more.

The next time someone comes back saying, "Forgive me, I broke your trust, give me one more chance," think twice — no, think thrice. Forgive them, because forgiveness is for *you,* not them. But never make the mistake of thinking things will go back to how they were. Once trust is broken, it's never the same. Once a snake bites you, you don't cuddle it again, right? Once a glass is shattered, no matter how much tape you use, it will never hold water again. Sure, you can tape it up and make it a showpiece — but it's never truly whole again.

And that's okay. Some things are meant to be lessons, not lifelines.

Okay you move on

Because staying stuck won't change what happened.
 Because the longer you stay in the past, the more you lose yourself.
 Because the people who hurt you aren't losing sleep over it — but you are.
 Because your life deserves more than sitting in old pain that's already done its damage.
 Because you deserve to heal, even if they never apologize.
 Because your future needs you more than your past does.
 Because there are better memories you haven't made yet.
 Because forgiveness is not for them — it's for you.
 Because carrying anger and sadness is like dragging a dead weight through your life.
 Because one day you will look back and wonder why you wasted so much time on something that was never meant to stay.
 Because peace is louder in silence than noise ever will be.
 Because real strength is not in holding on — it's in letting go and moving forward even with a broken heart.
 Because you're not weak for hurting — but you are powerful for choosing to rise after it.

You move on not because it's easy,
 but because you finally realize
 your heart is not a battlefield
 for people who never knew how to love it.

Imagine yourself just five years from now.
 Picture your grown-up self — stronger, wiser, busier, happier. Now ask yourself — won't your future self look back and wonder how you could be so stupid? How you kept waiting, crying, and breaking down for someone who doesn't even exist in your world anymore? Your future self will probably laugh at how immature you were, wasting all that precious time and energy on people you won't even have a phone number of, people who won't even cross your mind once.
 Don't disappoint the person you are becoming.
 Don't waste your today for someone who won't even matter in your tomorrow.

It's time you finally move on.
 No more wasting your time holding onto what was never meant to stay. Stop clinging to the past that's only holding you back. The people who walked away aren't coming back — and the ones who matter will never leave in the first place. It's not about erasing memories or pretending it never hurt. It's about choosing to no longer live in the shadows of what you've lost.Because you deserve a future where you're not defined by old wounds, a future where you're free to grow, to heal, to thrive. The longer you stay stuck, the more you lose sight of the life waiting for you.
 So, let it go. Let the hurt go. Let the anger go. Embrace the power that comes with walking away, with choosing yourself. Your peace, your happiness, and your future are worth so much more than any past pain.
 It's time. It's time to finally move on.

It's Time to Heal

I know this might sound strange — maybe even impossible —
but here's something we rarely talk about:
Moving on and healing are not the same.

You can move on with your life, go to school, laugh with
friends, post happy pictures, and still carry pieces of pain
you've buried deep.

 You can say "I'm over it" a hundred times and still flinch
when something reminds you of *that one memory*.
 Because healing doesn't happen just because time passed.
 Healing happens when you finally face what you've been
running from.

Here's one way to know the difference:
 When you've truly healed, you look back and smile — not
because it didn't hurt, but because it no longer controls you.
 You might even laugh at how much power you once gave
that moment, that person, that hurt.
 But when you haven't healed, you look back and feel the
same sting.
 You replay it, and instead of closure, you feel that lump in
your throat again.
 You think, "I didn't deserve that," and suddenly, your chest
feels heavy, your thoughts spiral, and you're back to
overthinking like it never left.

That's not healing.
That's surviving.

And while surviving is brave, **you deserve more than survival**.
You deserve freedom. You deserve peace. You deserve a life that doesn't carry pain in the background of every quiet moment.

Dont u think you have already given it a lot of time

And trust me — healing doesn't happen overnight. It's not something that just clicks one day and disappears the next. Healing is messy. It takes time. It takes learning how to control your thoughts when they try to drag you back into the same cycle of pain. It takes strength to hold yourself together when your emotions want to pull you apart.

Healing begins when you stop denying the reality and start accepting it. It starts the moment you stop expecting everything to go your way — when you realize that life doesn't always follow the script you had in mind. And that's okay. Because healing isn't about controlling the world around you — it's about learning to control how it affects you within.

It's high time you let yourself heal — not just pretend to. Walk with that bright smile, but this time, let it be real. Let it come from a place of peace, not performance. Do things your way. Live for yourself. Find joy in the small wins and take pride in how far you've come.

And promise me this — don't ever let your mental peace be shaken by people who don't know your heart. No matter how good you are, how honest or thoughtful, people will still talk. Some will misunderstand you. Some will judge. That's just life. But their noise doesn't define you. It never did.

What matters is how you carry yourself, how you rise above it, and how you protect your inner world from the chaos outside. You are allowed to take your time. You are allowed to fall and still choose to rise again. Just don't stop. Keep going. Keep healing. And most of all — keep choosing

When you wonder y it still hurts you when you have moved on why you feel like disappearing or erase that 1 incident from life i understand this but when you think practically you can never do this instead you heal

Healing doesn't happen for everyone — not because they don't want it, but because sometimes the pain feels safer than the unknown. But *you*, you are strong enough to choose healing. Not because you have to be perfect, but because healing is so much better than living in quiet breakdowns no one sees.

You *deserve* to heal.
You deserve peace.
You deserve to return to yourself — the calm, joyful, unapologetic version of you.

Don't hide behind a smile. Let your light speak for itself. Show the world that you are doing better, not because of them, but *despite* everything. Let them see how beautifully strong you've become.

Because you are **enough**, just the way you are

Healing isn't linear, and that's okay. It's not about rushing to "get better," but about letting the process unfold in its own time. There will be moments when you feel like you're moving backward, but that's just part of the journey. Growth often comes in unexpected bursts, and sometimes, it's the quiet, steady moments that make the most impact. Trust that you are healing, even when it doesn't feel like it. Every emotion, every tear, every laugh, and every setback is part of your transformation.

So, take your time. Don't pressure yourself to be "fixed" or to have it all figured out. Allow yourself the grace to be where you are. Embrace the process. You are worthy of healing, peace, and joy, even when it feels far away. You've come this far, and there's so much more strength within you than you know. Keep going—your journey is your own, and it's worth every step.

Remember, healing is not a race, and it doesn't happen on anyone else's timeline. You don't have to have all the answers right now, and that's perfectly okay. Every day, you are making progress, even if it feels like just a small step. Your heart is resilient, and your soul knows what it needs. Trust in that, and trust in yourself.

And above all— you should heal. You deserve it. You deserve to let go of the past that weighs you down and embrace the future with open arms. Healing is a gift to yourself, one that no one else can give you, but you can choose to give it to yourself every day. You are worth the time, the patience, and the peace that healing brings.

Being Alone Is Not Being Lonely

Sometimes, you need to walk alone — not because you're weak, but because healing demands it. Healing asks for silence. For stillness. For the kind of solitude where no one is watching, no one is judging, and no one is interrupting your process. You need time to breathe, to understand, to unlearn the noise and feel the truth in your bones. And in that quiet, something becomes painfully clear — if your absence doesn't affect someone, maybe your presence never really mattered to them in the way you thought it did.

We spend so much time trying to be there for people, trying to be enough, trying to please, and trying to fit in. We give pieces of ourselves, expecting that in return, we'll receive love, appreciation, or validation. And somehow, in that process, we begin to think that being alone means we're unwanted or unloved. But no — being alone is sometimes the first step toward truly being seen. Especially by yourself. Because before anyone else can value you, you need to value you. You need to understand the depth of your own worth, what you bring to the table, not just in love or friendships, but in your own personal journey.

There is strength in solitude, something that the world tends to overlook. Being alone isn't a sign of defeat; it's a sign of courage. Courage to face the raw parts of yourself that you've been avoiding. It's courage to sit with your pain and not run from it. It's courage to feel the weight of your emotions and know that you can stand tall even in their presence. In those moments of silence, you learn to listen to your own voice, to trust the rhythm of your heart, and to embrace the person you are, without needing anyone else to define you.

Being too available makes people forget your worth. And yes, that hurts — when you realise you were always the one reaching out, checking in, giving your all while getting crumbs in return. But healing... healing opens your eyes. It teaches you to stop begging to be understood. It shows you that not everyone deserves access to your softness. You are not supposed to be easily taken for granted. You are not a second choice. You are not someone to be loved only when it's convenient. You are a privilege.

When you start healing, you begin to hold that truth close. You stop oversharing. You learn to speak only when it's worth it. You become careful with your energy, your time, and your heart. You start protecting your peace like it's sacred — because it is. And most of all, you begin to understand the difference between being alone and being lonely.

Being alone is not being lonely.

It's choosing your own company over forced conversations. It's choosing clarity over chaos. It's finally having the space to hear your own voice without the noise of everyone else's opinions. It's waking up without anxiety about who will stay or leave — because for once, you've decided to stay with yourself.

Being alone is powerful. It's in the quiet nights and empty rooms that you begin to understand who you are. You begin to notice how resilient your heart really is. You start doing things you love, not to impress anyone, but because they fill your soul. You dance in your room, you read books that make you feel seen, you go on walks without needing company. You start healing not because someone else saved you, but because you did. And that — that's real strength.

In those silent battles, you realise it's not you vs. the world. It's you vs. you. The only real comparison that matters is who you were yesterday and who you're becoming today. Every small step you take, every boundary you set, every time you choose peace instead of reacting — that's you evolving. It's an ongoing process that doesn't need to be validated by others, because the only person you need to prove your growth to is yourself.

So tomorrow, when you wake up, ask yourself: *"How am I better than I was yesterday?"*

And let that answer guide your next move. Maybe today you'll smile a little more. Maybe you'll stop yourself from overthinking that one message. Maybe you'll finally set that boundary. Maybe you'll write a new page in your story. No matter how small the win, count it — because it matters.

Healing is not a straight path. It doesn't come with rules or timelines. Some days, you'll feel like you've made no progress at all. Other days, you'll feel invincible. But the beauty of it is in the messy middle. You'll have days when the pain comes rushing back, when the memories hit hard, when it feels like you're starting over. But that's okay. Growth is never linear. It's messy, it's confusing, and it's incredibly brave. You're becoming someone you've never been before — and that takes courage. You are learning how to hold space for your own transformation.

One day, you'll look back and smile at how far you've come. You'll laugh at what once made you cry. You'll thank yourself for walking away from what drained you. And most of all, you'll feel proud — because you healed. Not because someone fixed you, but because you finally chose you. And that choice, that act of choosing yourself over and over again, will be the greatest victory you'll ever experience.

So promise yourself this: Don't let the world convince you that needing space is weakness. Don't let anyone make you feel guilty for taking time to understand your emotions. Being alone is not punishment — it's preparation. It's power. It's where you remember who you were before the world told you who to be. It's where you start rewriting your own story.

You are not lonely. You are learning.

Learning to be okay without constant reassurance. Learning to shine without a spotlight. Learning to love without conditions. And above all, learning that your own company is enough — always has been, always will be.

We spend our lives searching for meaning in the world around us, trying to find answers in the places we think we should look: in others, in success, in possessions. But the truth is, the greatest discovery we'll ever make is not in what we find outside, but in what we uncover within. Because when we learn to embrace our own silence, when we listen to the whispers of our own hearts and minds, we begin to see that the answers were never hidden in the noise of the world. They've always been within us, waiting patiently for us to realize that the most profound journey is the one that leads us back to ourselves. And sometimes, the only thing we need to do to heal, to grow, to truly live, is to stop searching and simply begin to understand who we already are.

Bring Out the Real You

You know what? There's one quote that has kept me going all these years: "If it's not going to matter in the next five years, don't spend more than five minutes thinking about it." That one line has helped me breathe through storms, walk away from chaos, and find peace in things I can't control.

Now listen—maybe it's time to bring out the real you. The one hidden underneath all those layers of expectations, roles, and masks. Because let's be honest: who you are today might not be the real you. Have you noticed how you behave differently around different people? How you adjust yourself just to blend in, just to be the person they want you to be?

You try so hard to fit in, to become the most perfect person in someone else's life. But that's not how life works. Life isn't about pleasing everyone or molding yourself to fit someone else's version of "perfect."

Maybe you've found yourself in a group of friends who love gossiping or making fun of others, and even though it makes you uncomfortable, you laugh along just so you don't feel left out. Or maybe you dress a certain way, hold back your opinions, or pretend to like things you don't—just to be accepted.

Acting a certain way just to be accepted is exhausting. You know it. Putting on a mask every day, pretending to be someone you're not—it drains you. Why not just behave the way you want to? Do things that satisfy your soul, not society's standards. Be a trendsetter, not a copycat. The truth is, being real actually attracts the right kind of people—the ones who love you for who you truly are, not the version you pretend to be. And trust me, those are the people worth keeping.

It's really not easy—I understand. Good things take time, and real change doesn't happen overnight. But without taking that first small step, you're never really going to reach where you want to be. Waiting for the perfect moment or for everything to feel right will only keep you stuck. Growth begins the moment you decide to move, even if it's just one tiny step forward. You don't have to have it all figured out—just start.

And once you take that step, something shifts. You start feeling lighter. More *you*. Sure, not everyone will understand it. Some might even walk away. But that's okay. Let them. The people who are meant to be in your life will never ask you to dim your light just to make them comfortable.

You'll start to notice a difference—not just in how people see you, but in how you see yourself. Confidence doesn't come from perfection; it comes from being unapologetically real. From standing in front of the world and saying, "This is me. Take it or leave it."

And no, the road won't always be smooth. There will be days when you'll question everything. When self-doubt creeps in and the urge to go back to the "safe version" of you feels stronger than ever. But keep going. Remind yourself why you started. Reconnect with the fire that made you want to break free in the first place.

Because at the end of the day, the most powerful thing you can ever be is yourself. Not a version filtered by fear or shaped by opinions. Just you—raw, real, growing, glowing.

Start small. Speak up when something doesn't feel right. Say no when you need to. Stop apologizing for taking space.

Celebrate your wins, even the tiniest ones. That's how you build the real you—one decision at a time.

You don't have to be loud to be seen. You don't have to be perfect to be loved. You just have to be you. That's more than enough. And once you realize that, nothing can shake you. Not people's opinions. Not their silence. Not even your own fears.

So here's your reminder: You are allowed to grow. You are allowed to change. You are allowed to outgrow people, habits, and places. Don't cling to the version of you that made others comfortable. Evolve into the version that makes *you* proud.

The world doesn't need another copy. It needs the real you. The unfiltered, untamed, imperfectly perfect you.

Bring out the real you—and never hide again.

Because the moment you decide to live authentically, you give others permission to do the same. You become a light in a world full of masks. You become a safe space, a reminder, an example. And believe it or not, someone out there is waiting for *your* story to inspire theirs.

So wear your flaws like armor, your dreams like a crown, and your truth like a banner. Speak with honesty, walk with courage, and live with intention.

Let today be the day you stop shrinking. Let today be the day you choose freedom over fear. Let today be the day you bring out the real you—bold, brave, and beautifully yourself.

It's so easy to get caught up in trying to be who others expect you to be. Society, social media, your friends, and even family can sometimes create a version of you they want to see. But in the process, we lose track of who we truly are.

Now is the time to stop apologizing for being yourself. Stop dimming your light to fit into boxes others have created. It's okay to take up space. It's okay to make noise, to stand out, to be different. You were never meant to fit in. You were meant to stand out.

When you stop pretending to be someone else, you realize something important: being true to yourself not only sets you free, it also draws people to you who appreciate your authenticity. People who don't need you to change in order to love and respect you.

And let's be honest, everyone has their own insecurities. We all feel out of place sometimes, we all have fears, and we all struggle with self-doubt. The difference is in how we deal with those fears. Do you let them define you, or do you step forward anyway, despite them?

Real courage is not the absence of fear, but the willingness to act in spite of it. When you choose to be real, you make yourself vulnerable. You make yourself open to both the possibility of rejection and the beauty of connection. But you can't experience the latter if you never take the leap.

Yes, you'll stumble. You'll fall. You'll make mistakes. But you'll also rise. You'll learn. You'll grow. And with each misstep, you'll become stronger. You'll find that the more you let go of pretending to be perfect, the more you align with the real, powerful version of you. The one that's been waiting to come out.

So, what's stopping you?

Maybe you fear what people will think. Or perhaps you're afraid of standing out too much. But here's the thing: the moment you start living authentically, you'll realize that those who matter will embrace your truth. And those who don't? They're not the ones you need.

In a world full of people trying to be something they're not, the real you is a breath of fresh air. The people who are meant to be in your life will love you for exactly who you are, not the mask you put on. Don't waste your time worrying about the ones who don't appreciate the real you. They'll never understand, and that's okay.

You're not here to be everyone's cup of tea. You're here to be your own cup of whatever the heck you choose—bold, sweet, bitter, or strong. Let others sip what they want, and don't be afraid to embrace your flavor.

One of the most empowering things you can do for yourself is to stop seeking validation from others. Seek validation from within. The more you do this, the more you'll realize that you have everything you need to thrive inside of you already.

The world needs realness. It needs people who are unapologetically themselves. And guess what? That person is you. It always has been.

So here's your challenge: Start today. Start small, but start. Do one thing that is purely for you. Whether it's speaking your mind in a conversation, wearing what you truly love, or choosing the path less traveled, just start.

You are more than enough as you are. Don't wait for approval. Don't wait for the "perfect" time. The real you is here. And the world needs that version of you more than you realize.

Shape Your Real You

Okay you bought your real you out wow wonderful do you think Okay, you brought out the real you — wow, wonderful! But do you think your journey ends here? No, there's no chance. Now, it's like getting things ready to prepare a major feast.

Don't you feel you still have flaws?

Oh, I'm not telling you to be *perfect*.

Perfect people are never real, and real people are never perfect.

Yes, you've brought out the real you — but that doesn't mean you have to *like* everything you see. By this time, you may be feeling things like:
 "If only I was a little kinder..."
 "If I had been more mature and let karma do its thing..."

Listen to me — **it's not too late.**
 That doesn't mean you keep pushing it to tomorrow. If not today, then *when*?

You need to understand how you'll portray yourself to the world — not to please society, but to be **respected**. It's about bringing out the real you in a way that *you* like, a version that you're proud of.

Let me tell you a story

Once upon a time in a small village, there was a water bearer who had two pots. Each day, she carried them across her shoulders, down to the river and back to her home. One pot was perfect — it held all the water without spilling a drop. The other pot had a small crack and would leak water the entire journey back.

The cracked pot felt ashamed. "I'm useless," it said. "Because of me, you lose half the water every day."

The water bearer smiled gently. "Have you noticed the flowers along your side of the path and not the other?"

The pot paused. "No…"

"I planted seeds on your side," she said. "And every day, as we walked back, you watered them. You may be cracked, but you've brought beauty along the path. The other pot may be perfect, but you've been the one spreading life."

Moral:
 We all have flaws. But when we accept them, shape them, and walk with them — that's when we bring out the *real* us, the one who leaves behind trails of beauty.

Here is one more

There was this one girl — she always wished well for everyone around her. Her heart was big, and her smile was genuine. But over time, the chaos, the noise, the fights… it all got to her.

She became quiet.
 Nights turned into long cries.
 Sleep became a stranger.

There was one fight — one painful moment — that lingered in her mind like an echo she couldn't silence.

One night, while sitting in the dark, she asked herself:
 "Where is the inner child in me? The real me — the happy one?"

And a voice inside whispered back,
 "That's life, kiddo."

It hit her. She wasn't wrong for feeling too much.
 She realized she never hated anyone — she just stopped chasing the ones who didn't see her worth.

She began to gently distance herself from people who drained her.
 She stopped explaining her silence.
 She started working on her life.

And in that process, she met the **real her** again — the one who danced in quiet joy, who didn't need the world's noise to feel seen.

Once a talkative buddy, now a mature silence lover — not because she lost herself, but because she *finally found her.*

Moral:
 Sometimes, silence isn't sadness — it's healing.
 When you stop seeking validation from the wrong people and start valuing your own peace, you don't lose yourself…
 You *find* the version of you that was quietly waiting to be loved by *you.*

We often think becoming our "real self" is a destination. But it's not. It's a journey of unlearning the noise, the fear, the expectations — and rediscovering the version of ourselves that feels honest. It's in the choices we make every day — to walk away, to stand tall, to speak kindly, or stay silent with strength.

The real you doesn't come with perfection or applause. It comes with peace. It comes with choosing growth over grudges. And once you meet that version of you, trust me — you won't want to be anyone else again.

So go on, shape your real you — not to impress the world, but to finally come home to yourself.

It's okay if you're still figuring it all out. No one has the blueprint for life — we're all just building as we go. Some days, you'll feel on top of the world. Other days, you'll question everything. That's not weakness — that's being human. And being human means learning, stumbling, forgiving, and growing. Let yourself do that without guilt.

There will be people who misunderstand you, judge your silence, and question your change. Let them. You're not here to convince everyone that you're good. You're here to *become* good — for yourself. The real you doesn't need to shout to be seen. Real strength often walks in quietly and still leaves the biggest impact.

It's also okay to outgrow people, places, and even versions of yourself. Don't let loyalty to your past stop you from blooming into your future. You're not selfish for choosing peace. You're not cold for choosing space. You're just finally starting to value yourself the way you should have from the beginning.

Sometimes, healing feels like breaking. But those are the cracks that let the light in. Whether you're healing from friendships that faded or words that hurt deeper than anyone knows — remember: your emotions are valid. Your process is valid. The pace at which you grow is valid. And through it all, you are still worthy of love, respect, and joy.

So, if you're ever sitting with your thoughts, wondering if you're enough — I hope you remind yourself that you're not here to be perfect. You're here to be *real*. And the real you — with all your scars, strength, softness, and silence — is more than enough.

Who I Choose to Be

Just because you feel light—like a feather floating in the air—doesn't mean there's no room to grow. Feeling free is beautiful, but becoming who you truly want to be takes intention and effort. *Who you choose to be* isn't just about dreams; it's about decisions. Every thought, every action, every step forward shapes the person you're becoming.

See, who you want to be is completely your choice. No one else gets to decide that for you. Not your friends, not society, not even your past. It's in your hands. But let's be honest—there are moments when we forget that. Moments when we look at someone else and think, *"I wish I were like them."*

Maybe it was during a conversation when they spoke with so much confidence. Or maybe it was just watching them move through life, seemingly perfect. That quiet voice in your head starts whispering: *"Why can't I be like that?"* And just like that, doubt sneaks in. You start questioning yourself, your worth, your identity.

But nah, buddy—that's not how life works. You weren't meant to be a copy of someone else. You weren't made to blend in or to follow a script written for someone else's life. You were meant to stand out, to speak your truth, to be real.

Who you choose to be should come from within. The true you—flawed, beautiful, brave. Inside and out. It's time to stop pretending, to stop hiding behind who you think the world wants you to be. This is the moment where you stop shrinking and start becoming. Not someone else. Not a version edited by fear or pressure. But you.

Because at the end of the day, the most powerful, unstoppable, and honest thing you can ever be… is yourself.

Your life is like a tug of war—a constant pull between what society expects you to be and who you truly want to become. It's a battle between fitting in and standing out, between following the crowd and following your heart. And trust me, people will judge you no matter what. They'll talk behind your back whether you succeed or fail, whether you speak up or stay silent, even if you're practically perfect. That's just how people are. But remember this: *"Don't worry about the people who talk behind your back, they are behind for a reason "* Let them talk. Let them whisper. You just keep walking forward—toward the version of yourself you believe in.

So, when you stand in front of that mirror, ask yourself this: *Who do I want to be?* Not, *Who should I be?* Stop looking for answers in the world around you, because the truth is, no one else has the power to define your life. Not your friends. Not your family. Not society. *You* are the only one who can decide who you are and who you're becoming. It's your life, your choices, your identity.

For so long, you've looked for validation from others. You've tried to mold yourself into the version that they think is acceptable. But why? Why do you need their approval? Why have you spent so much of your energy trying to be what they expect of you, when the real question is, *Who are you trying to be for yourself?*

It's exhausting, isn't it? Trying to be someone you're not. Trying to please everyone except the one person who truly matters—you.

Look, you don't need their approval. You don't need anyone else's permission to live your truth. There will always be people who try to shape you into something that fits their narrative. But none of that matters if you're not living your own.

It's time to stop pretending. Stop shrinking your dreams to fit into their boxes. Stop dimming your light to make them feel comfortable. Because you're not meant to be small. You're not meant to hide. Who you choose to be is not about fitting into their perfect image of what they think you should look like or act like. It's about embracing your own flaws, your own quirks, your own struggles. It's about realizing that your imperfections are just as beautiful as your strengths.

It's about standing tall in your own skin, not because you're perfect, but because you're real. Because you've accepted every part of yourself, the good and the bad. It's about embracing your dreams, your fears, your passions, and your scars—all the pieces of you that make you uniquely, powerfully *you.* When you can finally look at yourself in the mirror and say, *"I am enough just as I am,"* you've won. That's when the transformation begins.

This is your journey. No one else's. You are the writer, the director, the star of your own story. You don't need to walk someone else's path. The world might tell you that you have to, but you get to decide. You're the one who has the power to choose your direction, to shape your future, to define who you're becoming.

So, stop worrying about who they want you to be. Stop living for their expectations. Stop worrying about whether they'll like you, accept you, or approve of you. The only approval you need is your own. You're the one who will have to live with your choices. You're the one who will carry the weight of your decisions. And trust me, it feels a whole lot lighter when you're being true to yourself.

The power has always been in your hands. It always will be. Every single day, you're given the opportunity to choose who you are. And no one can take that away from you, unless you let them. So stand tall, step forward, and decide. Choose to be the person you know you're meant to be. Not the person they want you to be. Not the person they expect you to be. But the person you were always meant to become.

"Stop living for their approval. Stop trying to fit into their boxes, to meet their expectations, to become someone you're not just to be liked. The truth is, they'll never understand the fire inside of you, because it's not meant to be contained. Your life is yours, and only you get to choose who you want to be. Not their whispers. Not their judgments. Not their idea of perfection. You are not here to fit their narrative—you are here to write your own story. Embrace every flaw, every fear, every dream, every scar. You are enough, just as you are, and the power to change your life, to shape your future, is in your hands. Own it. Choose it. Live it."

Time to Slay Life

You know, you've really come a long way. I mean, just look back—flip through the earlier pages of this book. It started with all that heaviness, the burden on your chest, the self-doubt that never seemed to end. You were carrying so much. You were trying so hard to be enough for everyone else that you forgot you were already more than enough for yourself. And now? Now you're peeling back the layers, finally meeting the *real* you—the one that's always been there, just waiting to be seen. Maybe it's still hard to fully believe it, maybe it still stings sometimes, but don't you feel it? That tiny shift inside? That growing spark?

This isn't just a book. It's a mirror. It's been quietly holding your hand, walking with you through the breakdowns, the breakthroughs, the heartbreaks, and the healing. And now it's telling you one thing—**it's time.** Time to stop tiptoeing around your worth. Time to stop apologizing for existing. Time to stop living in everyone else's shadows and finally step into your own damn light.

It's not selfish to choose yourself. Let me say that again—**it is not selfish to choose yourself.** This world has taught you to always give, always care, always worry about how others feel. But what about you? What about your joy? Your peace? Your dreams? You've cried enough tears. You've learned enough lessons the hard way. And now, you owe it to yourself to rise. Loud. Bold. Fearless.

It's time to slay life. Not just survive it. You've earned that crown through every silent battle you've fought. No more shrinking. No more second-guessing. No more waiting for the 'right time' to shine. This *is* the right time. This is your moment. Grab it with both hands, scream your name into the universe, and start living like the masterpiece you are.

THIS POEM IS SPECIALLY FOR YOU

You broke in silence, no one ever knew,
How many nights you wished the pain wasn't true.
But still—you rose, tear-stained and raw,
Not perfect, not whole, but stronger than before.

You stopped waiting for the world to clap,
And held your own hand through every collapse.
Because healing isn't loud, and growth isn't neat—
It's choosing to stand, when you barely have feet.

So now, you walk—not to impress, but to feel,
Not to prove, but to finally heal.
This life is yours, messy and bright—
You're not just surviving... you're stepping into your light.

It's not just about saying "this is your life" like it's some motivational quote you slap on a wall. No—it's deeper. It's about taking every heartbreak, every failure, every time you were made to feel like you weren't enough, and turning it into something that fuels you. It's about making peace with your past—not to forget it, but to learn from it. To build from it. Who you are today is not your final form. Picture yourself five years from now… still changing, still growing, still becoming. That version of you doesn't exist yet, but you're shaping them with every choice you make now. And if you've ever felt stuck or lost or small—please understand, *that's life*. We're all meant to outgrow versions of ourselves. Change isn't just natural—it's necessary. And it's beautiful.

But remember—life is short. And no, that's not just a saying, it's a reminder. A loud one. Every day you wake up is a chance, a miracle, a moment you'll never get back. So stop wasting your days trying to be what they expect. Stop shrinking yourself for people who wouldn't even notice if you disappeared. **Slay your life like it's your last chance to live it right.** Laugh loud. Cry if you need to. Love like your heart's never been broken. Chase what sets your soul on fire.

Because time… it's not a thing you own. It's borrowed. And how you spend it—that's your power. Invest it in people who light you up. In dreams that scare you. In a life that feels like it's yours. You don't owe this world perfection. You only owe yourself the courage to live *fully*. So, go on—slay your life. Loudly. Bravely. Unapologetically.

Let me tell you a small story

There was once a girl who used to dim her light—on purpose. Every time she walked into a room, she made herself smaller. She bit her tongue when she wanted to speak. She laughed softer so she wouldn't seem too loud. She wore clothes that didn't feel like her, spoke words that didn't come from her heart, and carried dreams she quietly buried because she thought they were "too much." People liked her that way. Quiet. Easy. Agreeable.

But what they never saw were the nights she cried alone in bed, asking herself, "Why can't I just be me?" She had this fire inside—bright, beautiful—but it was always smothered by the fear of judgment. She lived her life waiting for approval. For someone to tell her she was finally "enough."

Until one day, everything broke.

Not in some dramatic explosion—but quietly, in a moment of stillness. She looked in the mirror, tired eyes staring back, and whispered to herself, "I'm exhausted… of pretending." That was the moment something inside her shifted. She didn't scream. She didn't run. She just stood there… and decided she was done.

Done apologizing for her softness, her wildness, her dreams.

She started saying *no* when it hurt. She started wearing colors that made her feel alive. She wrote her name on blank pages like it mattered—because it did. People noticed. Some were shocked. Some walked away. But she kept going.

And day by day, she stopped living for the world—and started living for herself.

Now? She laughs with her whole chest. She cries when she needs to. She speaks up, even when her voice shakes. She slays life—not because it's perfect, but because it's finally hers.

And that's what this chapter is all about.

So here's your truth, plain and powerful—**you don't have to earn the right to be yourself.** You already are enough, just as you are, in every version you've ever been. The quiet one. The broken one. The blooming one. They all led you here. And from this point forward, you get to choose how your story unfolds. You get to choose bold over silent, whole over perfect, *you* over what the world expects. So wear your truth like armor. Shine without shame. And remember, you're not just walking through life anymore—you're owning it.

And SLAYING YOUR LIFE And SLAYING YOUR LIFE—on your own terms. No more edits. No more filters. Just raw, real, radiant *you*. Because this life? It's not waiting for permission. It's waiting for *you* to show up exactly as you are. So take up space. Take the leap. Take your power back.

You're not here to fit in—you're here to light it up. Keep rising, keep shining, and never forget: the world doesn't need a quieter version of you—it needs this you. The one who dares, the one who dreams, the one who *slays*.

Owning Your Story

There comes a time when you stop running.
From your past.
From your pain.
From the version of you that you once were.

And in that stillness, when the noise fades, you realize something powerful:
This is your story. All of it. Every scar. Every secret. Every silenced scream. Every lonely night. Every small win that no one noticed but you.

You've spent so long trying to rewrite yourself — to be smaller, quieter, easier to love.
You've apologized for being "too much," for feeling too deeply, for needing more than what people gave you. You've begged the world to see your heart, and when it didn't, you wondered if maybe your story just wasn't worth telling.

But here's the truth — you are the main character.
Not the sidekick. Not the filler character in someone else's plot.
You. Always you.

And main characters? They fall. They mess up. They cry.
But they always rise.

Sometimes we carry so much shame about what we've been through that we start to believe we are broken. Damaged. Unworthy of anything beautiful. But maybe — just maybe — the most beautiful things are built from pieces that were once shattered.

Own your heartbreak.
Own the way you trusted the wrong people.
Own the nights you screamed into pillows so no one would hear.
Own the days you smiled in front of everyone and collapsed behind closed doors.
Own the mistakes. Own the resilience. Own your healing.

Because healing isn't linear. It's not clean. It's messy.
Sometimes it looks like dancing at midnight and feeling free for the first time in weeks.
Other times it's lying on the bathroom floor wondering if you'll ever feel okay again.

And yet, you keep going. That alone makes you brave.

There is power in choosing to no longer be ashamed of who you were.
To say, *"Yes, I've been hurt. I've been angry. I've lashed out. I've given up. I've doubted myself. But I've also grown. I've loved deeply. I've held on. I've healed. I'm healing."*

You don't have to romanticize your pain. You don't have to turn it into poetry.
But you do have to own it. Because your story matters.
Not just the polished parts — but the messy middle, too.

People will try to rewrite your story for you. They'll tell you how you should have felt. What you should have done. Who you should be by now. But they don't get to hold the pen. You do.

So, write it your way.

Let your story scream, cry, laugh, break, and bloom.
Let it be chaotic and beautiful and unfinished.
Let it be yours.

Because when you own your story, you stop waiting for
someone to rescue you — and you realize… you've been the
hero all along.

And heroes?
They don't wear capes.
They wear scars.
And they walk forward anyway.

Main Character Affirmation:

"I am not my past. I am not my pain.
I am the author of my story.
I get to rise. I get to rewrite.
I am the main character —
and I choose to own every single page."

And so, let the world see you as you truly are:
Not perfect. Not flawless. But beautifully human.
Let them see you not in the light of your accomplishments
alone, but in the quiet moments where you chose to keep
going, even when everything seemed broken.
That's where your true strength lies.

You don't need anyone's permission to take ownership of
your life. Your story is yours, and there's power in that.
There's beauty in being the one who decides how it ends. And
the most powerful thing you can do is believe that no matter
what's happened, you're still worthy of your own love.

Your story is unfolding, and every page is a testament to your
resilience. You're not defined by the chapters you wish you

could rewrite, but by the strength you found in each moment
of doubt. Even when it felt like the end, it was just the
beginning of something new. You have everything within you
to keep writing — and to create the life you've always
dreamed of.

Remember, the journey isn't over. You are still growing, still
evolving, still becoming the person you were always meant to
be. So don't rush the process. Let each page turn in its own
time, and know that as you own your story, you're also
crafting the future that will rise from your past.

**"Your story isn't over, and you are the author of the next
chapter. Own every part of it, because you are the hero
who rises after every fall."**

Redefining Strength

You've been through so much, I know. There were days when the pain felt unbearable, when you questioned how much more you could take. But here you are, still standing. Even when you wanted to give up, something deep inside you kept pushing forward. It's not about how many times you fall; it's about how many times you rise. And with every rise, you grow stronger, even if you don't see it yet.

It's okay to feel tired. It's okay to feel weak sometimes. You've faced things that many wouldn't have had the courage to even look at. Yet, you've carried on — even when it felt like your world was collapsing around you. You've weathered storms that most people wouldn't survive. You are still here, and that alone speaks volumes about your strength.

But here's the thing — you are not just surviving anymore. You're living. And it's time to redefine what strength truly means for you. Because the version of strength you held onto before was a survivor's strength — a strength built out of necessity, out of sheer willpower to keep going. But now, you've grown. Now, your strength is something else. It's no longer just about making it through the day. It's about thriving, growing, and embracing the person you've become.

Strength is not about how many punches you can take before you break. It's about how you stand tall after each one. It's about knowing that the battles you face don't define you — they shape you. Every hardship you've endured has built something inside you, something stronger than you could have imagined. Every tear you've shed has watered the seeds of resilience. And now, you're not just surviving; you're evolving.

If you're studying, your strength is in the dedication, the perseverance, the long nights when you feel like giving up. It's in the moments when you push through the exhaustion, when you remind yourself that you are capable, even when doubts plague your mind. You find strength in your commitment to your goals, even when the pressure seems overwhelming. Every challenge you face, every test you tackle, is a chance to show yourself that you are worthy of success. And when you rise to the top — it's not just about the grades or the recognition. It's about the quiet confidence you gain in knowing that you can do anything you set your mind to.

If you're working, your strength is in the way you take on responsibilities, even when it feels like you're drowning in tasks. It's in your ability to remain calm under pressure, to find solutions when everything seems chaotic. You've learned how to juggle multiple roles, how to wear many hats, and still remain standing. Your strength is found in your ability to keep moving forward, no matter how overwhelming life gets. And when you complete a project, when you achieve a goal, it's not just about the end result. It's about the person you become in the process — someone who's learned to handle pressure with grace, who's learned to turn challenges into opportunities.

But strength isn't just about achievements. It's about how you show up when no one is watching. It's in the way you love others, even when your own heart is broken. You've been a good daughter, a good son, a good friend. You've given everything to the people you love — and sometimes, that's meant putting your own needs on hold. But it's time to realize that your strength lies not just in your sacrifices, but in your ability to love and care for yourself too. You've spent so much time pouring into others, but now it's time to pour into you. It's time to stop being the only one holding up the world and start allowing yourself to be held.

You may not always feel strong. There are days when the weight of everything can feel like it's too much. There are days when you wonder if you can keep going. But in those moments, you must remember that strength isn't about being invincible. Strength is about vulnerability. It's about allowing yourself to feel the pain, to acknowledge your struggles, and still choosing to rise. It's in the moments when you're on your knees, when you feel broken, and yet you gather the courage to stand back up.

You have been through things that would have destroyed others, but you're still here. And that, my friend, is strength. It's not in the victories you've won or the goals you've reached — it's in your ability to keep going when everything else tells you to quit. You've survived the worst, and now you're learning how to thrive.

You've been through heartbreaks, losses, and disappointments, and yet you're here. And that's where your strength lies — in the fact that you never gave up. You kept going, even when it felt like you had nothing left. Your strength is not just in the battles you've fought, but in the courage it took to keep fighting, to keep going, even when you didn't think you could.

And now, it's time to redefine what strength means for you. Strength is not about how much you can endure. It's about how you rise after every fall. It's about knowing that you are strong enough to survive, and brave enough to live fully. Strength is about learning to trust yourself, to believe in your own power. It's about looking at the scars of your past and realizing they are the markers of your strength, not your weakness. It's about owning your story, your journey, and understanding that you are stronger than you ever gave yourself credit for.

You may not always see it. You may not always feel it. But every day, you grow stronger. Every time you rise after falling, you grow more powerful. And every time you keep moving forward, despite the odds, you become the person you were always meant to be.

So, redefine your strength. Know that it is not about how much you can carry, but about how much you can rise. Every time you get knocked down, you have the choice to rise up even stronger. That is your true power. That is your strength.

You are stronger than you think. And you always have been.

Quote for Reflection:

"Strength is not about how much you can endure, but about how you rise every time you fall. It's in the quiet courage to keep going when everything around you seems impossible."

Nurturing Inner Peace

In a world full of noise, deadlines, expectations, and constant comparisons, finding a moment of silence within can feel almost impossible. But that moment—the one where you feel calm, grounded, and okay just being you—is what we call **inner peace**. And nurturing it is not just important; it's essential.

What is Inner Peace?

Inner peace is not about being calm only when everything around you is calm. It's about staying steady even when life is stormy. It's a mental and emotional state where you feel balanced, calm, and centered, no matter what's happening on the outside. It's not the absence of problems, but the presence of strength and clarity in facing them.

People who nurture inner peace are not free from stress or sadness—they just learn how to handle these emotions without letting them control their lives.

Why Is It Important?

Without inner peace, stress takes over. Small problems feel like mountains. Relationships suffer. You may even lose sight of who you truly are. But with inner peace, you gain emotional strength. You learn to respond, not react. You become your own anchor in the middle of a storm.

How to Nurture Inner Peace?

Just like plants need water, sunlight, and care to grow, inner peace needs regular attention. Here are some gentle ways to nurture it:

1. Practice Mindfulness

Pay attention to the present moment. Let go of the past and don't rush to the future. Whether it's eating, walking, or simply breathing, be fully there.

2. Set Healthy Boundaries

Not every message needs a reply. Not every fight is worth your energy. Protect your space. Say no when something doesn't feel right.

3. Let Go of Control

You cannot control how others act, but you can control how you respond. Accept what you can't change and focus on what you can.

4. Be Kind to Yourself

Talk to yourself the way you would to a best friend. Forgive yourself for mistakes. You're human, and that's okay.

5. Connect with Nature

Spend time in green spaces. Listen to the sound of the wind. Watch the clouds move. Nature has a quiet way of healing.

6. Limit Negativity

Reduce exposure to toxic news, social media drama, and negative self-talk. Create a positive environment—both inside and out.

A Real-Life Story: Mahatma Gandhi's Inner Peace

Mahatma Gandhi, one of the greatest leaders the world has ever seen, lived a life filled with struggle, pressure, and opposition. But through it all, he stayed deeply peaceful within himself. Gandhi believed that true strength comes from inner calmness, not from shouting, fighting, or forcing others to listen.

When he was in South Africa, Gandhi was thrown off a train just because of the color of his skin. Most people would have been angry, but Gandhi chose a different path. He reflected quietly and decided to fight injustice with non-violence and truth.

He later led India's freedom movement not with guns or hatred, but with peaceful protests. Even when he was jailed or beaten, he never raised his voice in anger. Instead, he spent time meditating, praying, spinning cotton, and writing letters. He believed in the power of silence. In fact, Gandhi observed a day of complete silence every week, using that time to reconnect with his soul and reflect on life.

When India finally became free in 1947, Gandhi was heartbroken to see people fighting each other during Partition. While the country celebrated independence, Gandhi chose to fast and pray for peace. He walked among people, urging them to see each other as brothers and sisters, not enemies.

He once said, *"You may never know what results come of your actions. But if you do nothing, there will be no result."* Even in his final moments, after being shot, Gandhi whispered a prayer—"Hey Ram"—showing that his mind was at peace, even in pain.

His life teaches us that inner peace is not weakness—it is real power. It is the ability to stand strong with love and calmness, even when the world is falling apart.

There's a place inside I rarely show,
 A quiet ache I've come to know.
 Not loud like pain, nor sharp like fear,
 But a silent wish to disappear.

I smile, I laugh, I wear the face,
 But deep within, I miss the grace—
 The gentle voice that used to guide,
 Before the noise, before I cried.

I've searched the world for something whole,
 To fill the cracks, to calm my soul.
 But peace, it seems, won't shout or chase—
 It waits for me in empty space.

In tear-streaked nights and broken prayer,
 It wraps around my need for air.
 Not to erase what hurt has done,
 But to remind me—I'm not undone.

I learn to breathe, not just survive,
 To sit in silence and feel alive.
 To hold my wounds, not run or hide—
 To find the stillness deep inside.

It doesn't ask for perfect parts,
 Just open hands and softer hearts.
 And in that quiet, slow release,
 I meet myself—and I find peace.

Living Authentically

In the whirlwind of life, amid expectations, pressures, and a thousand voices telling us who to be, there is a quiet, unwavering truth that lives within us all—our authentic self. To live authentically is to step into the world exactly as you are, without pretenses, without fear of judgment, and without the desire to please others. It is about letting go of the roles we've been forced to play and discovering the person we've always been underneath.

Living authentically is not a destination—it's a journey. A journey of discovering, accepting, and embracing who we truly are, flaws and all. It's about peeling back layers of social conditioning, expectations, and fears, and reconnecting with the core of who we were before the world told us how to be.

From the time we are born, we are shaped by the world around us—by our families, schools, communities, and society. We are taught to follow certain paths, to fit into boxes, to be "good," "successful," and "acceptable." In the process, we often lose touch with our true selves, taking on identities that aren't ours but the ones the world wants for us. We begin to mold ourselves into something we think others will love or approve of, forgetting that the person we need to love most is *ourselves*.

For most of us, this is a quiet struggle. We may not even notice it at first. It's a soft, persistent whisper in our minds, telling us that something isn't quite right. We feel disconnected from our own desires, emotions, and dreams. We follow paths laid out by others because they seem easier or more "acceptable." But inside, we feel a longing—a yearning for something more. We begin to ask ourselves, *Is this really me? Is this what I want?*

The journey toward authenticity is not always straightforward. It involves moments of doubt, of fear, of confusion. It means stripping away the masks we wear to fit in and standing face-to-face with the real person we've always been. It means showing up in the world as we are, without pretending, without hiding, and without apology. And that takes courage.

True authenticity is not the absence of fear—it's the ability to act despite it. It's about making choices based on what feels right deep within, even if those choices aren't popular or easy. It's about embracing your flaws and imperfections, understanding that they don't make you less than, but part of your unique beauty. It's about being comfortable with your own voice, even if it shakes. It's about living with integrity, speaking your truth, and allowing others to do the same.

One of the most inspiring examples of living authentically in the public eye is Emma Watson. A household name for her role as Hermione Granger in the *Harry Potter* series, Emma's life could have easily been defined by her fame, by the public's expectations of her, and by the roles she was expected to play. But instead, Emma chose to use her platform for something far greater than personal success. She became a passionate advocate for gender equality and women's rights, stepping into the role of a UN Women Goodwill Ambassador.

When Emma Watson began speaking out for women's rights, she didn't do so because it was easy. She didn't do it to gain more popularity or approval. She did it because it aligned with her authentic self—her true values. She was speaking about something that mattered deeply to her, even if it made people uncomfortable or if they judged her for being "too political" or "too outspoken." Through her journey, Emma has shown that being authentic means standing up for what you believe in—even if the world questions you for it.

What's remarkable about Emma Watson's authenticity is that she doesn't just speak her truth; she lives it. She doesn't try to hide the fact that she, too, struggles with insecurities or imperfections. She openly speaks about the challenges of being both a public figure and a passionate advocate for change. She allows herself to be vulnerable, and in doing so, she connects deeply with others who are also learning to embrace their own authenticity.

Living authentically requires vulnerability, and vulnerability is often seen as a weakness. Society teaches us that we must be strong, perfect, and put together at all times. But the truth is, it's our vulnerability that connects us to others. It's in our moments of weakness, our honesty, and our willingness to expose our true selves that we allow others to see the real us—and in return, we give them permission to do the same.

Living authentically also means letting go of the fear of judgment. It's understanding that not everyone will like you, and that's okay. Authenticity is not about seeking validation from others; it's about validating yourself. It's about knowing that you are enough, exactly as you are, without needing to change for anyone else.

This journey toward living authentically is not always easy, especially when we face external pressures to conform. But it is, without a doubt, worth it. When we embrace who we truly are, we find a deep sense of peace and fulfillment. We stop living for the approval of others and start living for our own happiness, growth, and self-respect.

There will be days when the world feels overwhelming, when it seems easier to slip into the comfort of pretending. There will be times when the desire to fit in is strong, and you will feel the pull of being "someone else" for the sake of acceptance. But remember this: You were never meant to be someone else.

You are enough as you are. Your thoughts, your dreams, your quirks, your flaws—all of it makes you who you are. When you embrace your authenticity, you step into your power. You step into your true self, and from that place, you can create, love, grow, and thrive.

As the renowned author Brené Brown beautifully put it:

> *"Authenticity is the daily practice of letting go of who we think we're supposed to be and embracing who we are."*

Living authentically is a journey. It's not always a smooth path, and it's not without its challenges. But it is the only path that leads to true fulfillment. When you walk this path, you are no longer chasing approval or pretending to be someone you're not. You are simply being you—the way you were always meant to be.

So, don't be afraid to stand tall in your truth. Don't be afraid to let go of the mask. Live authentically, for that is where the magic happens. Live as you are—because there is no one else who can do that better than you.

Manifesting Your Future

Have you ever heard of vision boards or manifestation? When I first heard about them, it honestly sounded a bit silly to me. The idea that a simple picture or affirmation could shape your future didn't make sense at first. But then, something surprising happened in my own life, something that made me realize just how powerful these practices can be—especially when you combine them with hard work and consistency.

Let me take you back to my school days. Back then, I was struggling with a lot of personal challenges. There were friendships falling apart, a lot of confusion, and a sense of not knowing where I fit in. My 9th final exams were fast approaching, and the pressure was unbearable. I could feel the weight of expectations bearing down on me. It was a tough time emotionally, and to be honest, I didn't feel like I had the strength to deal with everything happening around me.

But there was this one thing that stuck with me during that time. It was something I didn't even realize I was using to change my mindset. I had this wallpaper on my phone that said, "PROVE THEM WRONG." It wasn't some deep philosophical mantra, nor was it a grand quote that promised life-altering transformation. It was simple, almost blunt, but it resonated with me in a way I didn't fully understand at the time.

Every time I looked at my phone, that message would stare back at me, like a reminder—not to prove anything to anyone else, but to prove it to myself. It gave me a sense of purpose, a reason to push through the obstacles I was facing, whether they were academic struggles or personal doubts.

It wasn't just a wallpaper on my phone—it became a silent motivator. Without even realizing it, I was manifesting success in my own life. I worked day and night, pouring myself into my studies. The pressure from the final exams was still there, but now, I was fueled by something deeper. That simple phrase pushed me to show up, to do the work, and to believe in myself, even when I felt like giving up.

When I look back at that time now, I realize that manifesting doesn't always have to be some grand or mystical process. It doesn't have to involve some elaborate ritual or a magical shift in energy. Sometimes, it's as simple as a small thought, a phrase, or a vision that keeps you focused on your goals. And when you align that with consistent effort, manifestation becomes less about magical thinking and more about dedication.

At first, the idea of manifesting felt a bit silly to me. I thought, "How could thinking about something make it happen?" But what I came to understand is that it wasn't just the thinking that worked. It was the belief behind the thinking, the action that followed the intention, and the consistency that turned a simple message into a reality.

That wallpaper was a visual reminder of what I wanted—good marks, not for anyone else, but for my own peace of mind, my own confidence. It made me realize that manifestation isn't about wishing for things to magically fall into place. It's about setting your mindset in a direction and taking consistent action toward your goal. It's about making a choice every day to show up, even when it's hard.

Manifesting became my way of aligning my thoughts with my actions. Every time I saw that message, I was reminded to keep pushing, to keep studying, and to believe that I could make it. It wasn't about relying solely on a wallpaper or some abstract idea; it was about trusting myself enough to keep going, even when the path seemed tough. And that's when it hit me: the true magic of manifestation lies in consistency.

I think what I learned most from that experience was that we have so much more power than we often give ourselves credit for. We can shape our future by aligning our thoughts, actions, and beliefs. That message, simple as it was, helped me focus on what I could control: my effort, my persistence, and my belief in my ability to succeed.

So, whether or not you believe in the power of vision boards or manifesting, there's one undeniable truth that I learned from my own experience: Consistency is key. It's not about one magical moment or a sudden shift in energy; it's about showing up every day, putting in the work, and believing that your efforts will lead to something meaningful.

When I finally received the results of my exams, I knew I had earned every mark. The journey wasn't easy, but it was worth it. That simple phrase, "PROVE THEM WRONG," had turned into a reminder that I could prove to myself that I was capable of more than I had ever believed.

The power of manifestation isn't just about wishing for success; it's about creating the conditions for success through focus, effort, and consistency. And sometimes, all it takes is a small visual cue, like a wallpaper, to remind you of what you're capable of and to keep pushing you toward your dreams.

So, if you ever feel lost or uncertain about the path ahead, remember this: Manifest your future by believing in yourself, staying consistent, and trusting the process. Your future is yours to create, and sometimes, all it takes is a little reminder to help you stay focused on the incredible journey that lies ahead.

In the end, I've come to realize that manifestation isn't about waiting for things to magically happen. It's about taking control of your mindset, aligning your intentions with consistent action, and trusting in your ability to shape your own future. That simple phrase on my phone wasn't a shortcut to success; it was a tool that helped me focus, stay motivated, and keep going even when things felt overwhelming. So, if you ever doubt the power of small reminders, visual cues, or positive affirmations, remember that they can be the spark that keeps you moving forward. It's your effort, persistence, and belief that turn dreams into reality. Keep believing in yourself, keep showing up, and watch your hard work transform into the success you've always dreamed of.

The Power of Moving Forward

There are times in life when it feels like the world is closing in, when the weight of every failure, every mistake, and every broken dream seems too much to bear. The days blur together, and you start to wonder if you'll ever find your way out of the maze of uncertainty and doubt. Those moments are hard. They leave you questioning yourself, your path, and your worth. But amidst the chaos, there's one truth I've learned: the power of moving forward is often what pulls us from the darkest places, even when we can't see the light at the end of the tunnel.

I remember a time when I felt lost—when I was overwhelmed by the pressure of school, the expectations of others, and the weight of my own insecurities. There were days when I felt like I wasn't good enough, that I would never be able to meet the standards that had been set for me. I wasn't just struggling academically—I was struggling emotionally. Friendships seemed fragile, and I questioned where I truly belonged. It felt like the harder I tried, the more everything slipped out of my grasp. It was during those times, when everything seemed to be falling apart, that I discovered the most important lesson I would ever learn: moving forward, no matter how small the steps, is what keeps you going.

It wasn't some grand moment of realization, nor was it an overnight shift in perspective. It happened slowly, almost imperceptibly. It started with something as simple as a phrase—a phrase that I placed as my wallpaper on my phone:

"PROVE THEM WRONG." I'll admit, when I first saw it, I thought it was a bit too blunt, too simple to hold any real power. How could such a small phrase possibly change anything? But what I didn't understand at the time was that this phrase wasn't just a reminder to prove anyone else wrong—it was a call to prove to myself that I was capable, that I had the strength to push through, no matter how difficult the journey seemed.

Every time I saw that message on my phone, something shifted inside me. It wasn't about showing off to the world or trying to make anyone believe in me—it was about showing up for myself, about proving to myself that I had the ability to keep going, even when the road ahead felt impossible. And slowly, as I continued to see that message day after day, something changed. I started believing it. I started believing in myself. That phrase gave me the strength to keep going, to keep pushing, even when everything inside me was telling me to quit.

But the true power of moving forward doesn't lie in the belief alone. It lies in the action. It lies in the small, consistent steps we take each day, even when we feel like nothing is changing. And it's in those small steps that something magical happens. The weight of our challenges doesn't feel as heavy when we're moving forward. The pressure doesn't feel as suffocating when we choose to take action instead of being paralyzed by fear or doubt. Moving forward doesn't mean ignoring the obstacles or pretending they don't exist. It means acknowledging them and choosing to keep going despite them.

There were days when I didn't feel like studying. There were nights when I didn't feel like trying, when the exhaustion seemed too much to bear. But every time I looked at that phrase—every time I remembered what it meant to prove myself wrong—I found the strength to keep going. I took one step. And then another. And slowly, without even realizing it, I began to see progress. It wasn't about an immediate transformation, but about the small victories along the way—the late nights spent studying, the hours spent working through my doubts, the quiet moments when I chose to keep going, even when it felt like nothing would ever change.

And when the day of my exams finally arrived, I realized something I hadn't expected: I had done the work. I had put in the effort, I had fought through the doubts, and I had kept moving forward. The results weren't just a reflection of my knowledge—they were a reflection of my persistence, my ability to keep going when it felt like the world was against me. That simple phrase, "PROVE THEM WRONG," had helped me tap into a power I didn't even know I had. It wasn't just about the grades—it was about proving to myself that I was capable of more than I ever thought possible.

Looking back now, I realize that moving forward isn't about perfection. It's about progress. It's about showing up, even when it's hard. It's about taking those small steps, no matter how insignificant they may seem, because each step brings you closer to the person you're meant to be. It's about trusting the process, even when the outcome is unclear. It's about knowing that every single day, every single choice, is shaping the future you want to create.

The road ahead will never be without challenges. There will always be moments of doubt, of fear, and of uncertainty. But in those moments, remember that the power lies not in waiting for things to change, but in continuing to move forward. It's not about taking huge leaps or achieving everything all at once—it's about taking those small steps, over and over again, with consistency and belief.

When you feel lost or unsure of the path ahead, know this: you have the strength to keep moving forward. You have the power to create your future, not with grand gestures or magic, but with the small, everyday actions that make up your journey. The key is in staying consistent, in trusting yourself, and in believing that every step, no matter how small, is bringing you closer to where you need to be.

So, if you ever find yourself at a crossroads, unsure of which way to go, remember this: the power of moving forward is always in your hands. It's not about waiting for the perfect moment—it's about making the choice to keep going, no matter what. Your future is waiting, and the only way to reach it is by continuing on the path, step by step, with unwavering belief in yourself and your ability to overcome anything that stands in your way.

In the end, moving forward isn't just about reaching a destination—it's about becoming the person you were always meant to be along the way.

Final Thoughts

As we come to the end of this journey, I want to leave you with one final thought. This book has been a reflection of the challenges we face, the growth we experience, and the strength we find within ourselves when we are determined to move forward. We've traveled through the highs and lows, the moments of doubt and triumph, and we've witnessed the profound truth that the power to shape our future lies not in waiting for things to magically fall into place but in consistently showing up, in putting in the effort, and in believing that, no matter the obstacles, we can move forward.

It's a reminder that life will never be without challenges, but it's how we choose to meet those challenges that truly defines us. Each day, we are faced with choices—whether to give up or to keep going, whether to let fear control us or to trust in our own strength. And it's in the moments when we choose to keep moving forward that we discover who we truly are and what we are capable of.

I hope this book has been a source of inspiration and comfort to you, reminding you that no matter where you are in life, you have the power to change your story. Don't be afraid to dream big, to fail, and to try again. Trust in yourself, trust in the process, and most importantly, trust that every step you take, no matter how small, is leading you to a brighter, stronger, and more confident version of yourself.

Thank you for taking this journey with me. Your story is still being written, and I believe that the best chapters are still ahead. Keep moving forward.

With love and belief in your potential,

Smina Jain

About the Author

Smina Jain, born on 18th November 2009, is a young writer and thinker who wants to make a change in the world. She believes in the power of small steps to create big personal growth. Along with her passion for writing, Smina enjoys exploring science, painting, and spending time with her friends. Through this book, she hopes to inspire readers to take action and become the best versions of themselves.

A Personal Message from the Author

There was a time in my life filled with long periods of silence and many nights spent crying alone, struggling to understand my feelings and the challenges I faced. During those quiet moments, I began to see things more clearly — about myself, about pain, and about the power we all have to change. It wasn't easy, but slowly, I started to understand that even small steps can make a big difference.

I chose to write this book because I know how hard it can be to face those dark moments alone. If my experiences and the lessons I've learned can help even one person going through similar struggles, then this book will have served its purpose. My hope is that these pages offer comfort, strength, and practical guidance, so no one feels lost or hopeless.

Life isn't perfect, and change doesn't happen overnight, but with patience and courage, we can all take steps toward a better tomorrow. This book is my way of reaching out, sharing what I've learned, and encouraging you to believe in your own power to grow and heal.